C000132886

Galatians
FOR BEGINNERS

MIKE MAZZALONGO

THE "FOR BEGINNERS" SERIES

The "For Beginners" series of video classes and books provide a non-technical and easy to understand presentation of Bible books and topics that are rich in information and application for the beginner as well as the mature Bible student.

For more information about these books, CDs and DVDs visit: **bibletalk.tv/for-beginners**

Copyright © 2015 by Mike Mazzalongo

ISBN: 978-0692421284

BibleTalk Books
14998 E. Reno
Choctaw, Oklahoma 73020

Scripture quotations taken from the New American Standard Bible®, Copyright © 1960, 1962, 1963, 1968, 1971, 1972, 1973, 1975, 1977, 1995 by The Lockman Foundation Used by permission. (www.Lockman.org)

TABLE OF CONTENTS

1.
INTRODUCTION TO GALATIANS

One of the first attacks against Christianity came directly against the gospel itself from people within the church. The attack came from Jewish Christians who began to insist that Gentiles (non-Jews) who wanted to become Christians had to become Jews first, before becoming Christians. This meant that for a Gentile to become a Christian, he first had to be circumcised and then he would be baptized.

Gentile Christians in the region of Galatia were being influenced by this pressure, and so Paul the Apostle writes this epistle in response to the problems caused by this teaching.

In the study of this epistle we will:

1. Examine the implications and dangers of this teaching for the Galatians as well as every generation faced with similar ideas.

2. Review Paul's teaching on the doctrine of "justification by faith" which is the heart of the gospel.

3. Study the true meaning of freedom and how it is expressed in Christian lives.

4. Learn about Paul's early life as a Christian.

Background of the Epistle – Galatians

Galatia was a Roman province in Asia Minor. The letter to the Galatians was addressed to the cities in the southern part of Galatia where Paul had established several congregations on his first missionary journey. There are four that we know of, all established between 44 and 47 AD in what is known as modern day Turkey.

- Antioch – Acts 13:14
- Iconium – Acts 13:51
- Lystra – Acts 14:8
- Derbe – Acts 14:19-21

As Luke tells the story in Acts 13:42-51, the Jews were happy to hear the good news of Christ. These Jews who were scattered throughout the Roman Empire were pleased to receive Paul and hear of the coming of the Messiah.

They became offended and jealous however, when they realized that the Gentiles (non-Jews of any nationality) were included in the promise of God and were accepting Christ in great numbers. This protest by the Jews took the form of a group that insisted that if the Gentiles were to become Christians, they had to first obey Jewish laws and customs to earn that right. This probably involved circumcision and obedience to food laws and various Jewish religious customs.

Upon his return to Jerusalem from that region, in order to report on his ministry, Paul was faced with a backlash in the form of a group within the church referred to as the Circumcision Party. They were known as this because of their insistence that all Gentiles be circumcised before they became Christians, or else be denied the opportunity.

In Acts 15:1-77 we read about Paul and the other Apostles, as well as the elders of the church in Jerusalem, discussing and trying to resolve this matter. At this meeting Paul recounts the blessings and power God gave him in preaching to the Gentiles, and that his ministry among them was legitimately ordained by God. Peter also stood with Paul and confirmed that Paul had indeed been sent specifically by God's command. James proposed that they write a letter to the church (the Gentiles) confirming Paul's ministry among them and reassuring them that they need not be troubled by any requirement to be circumcised. This letter was delivered to the church at Antioch, not in Galatia.

The letter to the Galatians was written soon after this meeting (50-51 AD) and is one of, if not the earliest, the New Testament books to be written and circulated.

The objective that Paul is trying to accomplish with this letter is to explain to the Galatians that:

1. The blessings that accompany salvation were earned by Christ's perfect faith and obedience.

2. We obtain these blessings because we are associated, or united, or identified to Christ by faith, which is expressed in baptism and obedience to His Word, not just intellectual affirmation.

3. We cannot earn blessings by works of the Law, ceremony or benevolence apart from Christ.

4. Those who try will fail and be condemned.

Outline

- Greeting – 1:1-5
- Rebuke – 1:6-9
- Personal History
  - Conversation and Early Years – 1:10-17
  - First Meeting with Peter – 1:18-24
  - Second Meeting with Peter – 2:1-10
  - Third Meeting with Peter – 2:11-14
- Discourse on Justification by Faith
  - Righteousness comes by Faith – 2:15-21
  - Spirit and Power comes by Faith – 3:1-5
  - Inheritance of Abraham come by faith – 3:6-29
  - Sonship comes by Faith – 4:1-7
  - Freedom comes by Faith – 4:8-31
- Exhortations
  - Exhortation to Stand Firm in Freedom
    1. Reject Circumcision – 5:1-12
    2. Love One Another – 5:13-15
    3. Walk by the Spirit – 5:16-24
    4. Encourage One Another – 5:25-6:5
    5. Help One Another – 6:6-10
- Final Warning Against False Teachers and Salutation
  - Warning Against Circumcision Party – 6:11-16
  - Salutations – 6:17-18

Greeting - 1:1-15

> [1] Paul, an apostle (not sent from men nor through the agency of man, but through Jesus Christ and God the Father, who raised Him from the dead),

Paul reaffirms his position as Apostle because the Judaizers (Circumcision Party), in questioning the gospel to the Gentiles, were also questioning his Apostleship. He did this in letters where his authority was questioned or where he was unknown (Romans, I and II Corinthians, Ephesians and Colossians), but refrained in churches where he was accepted (Philippians and I and II Thessalonians).

He reminds them first of all that his Apostleship was received from Christ and God in the same way as the other Apostles received their Apostleship. He also states that he was not appointed by the church council (Acts 15), nor was he appointed by Peter to become an Apostle.

Apostleship gave one the right to speak with authority in Christ's name and Paul claims this authority based on his legitimate and genuine Apostleship received from Christ (unlike the Judaizers who could not make this claim). Paul does not deny the Apostleship of others, but does not recognize any authority over him by any other group or Apostle, except the gospel of Christ.

His reference to the resurrection is the mark of the true Apostle, the personal witness of this event. He mentions it not as doctrine, but as one who confirms this doctrine as a chosen eyewitness.

> [2] and all the brethren who are with me,
> To the churches of Galatia:

We do not know who the "brothers with him" are, only that they share in the greeting. Paul reserves the title "churches in God or Christ" in addressing the Galatians since they are on the road to apostasy. He merely refers to them as churches located in Galatia, those he formed earlier in Iconium, Lystra, Derbe and Antioch.

> [3] Grace to you and peace from God our Father and the Lord Jesus Christ, [4] who gave Himself for our sins so that He might rescue us from this present evil age, according to the will of our God and Father

Paul offers a usual blessing that they receive favors from God and the peace that comes with it. This favor and peace is connected to Jesus Christ of whom Paul says two things:

1. He is Lord. Here, Paul uses a term to signify Deity and equality with God. The term "kurios" originally had secondary meanings, but the Jews and later the Apostles and disciples came to use it when referring to Jesus and His divinity.

2. Paul reviews the work of salvation accomplished by Christ and its ultimate results:

   o Christ offers Himself as a sacrifice for sins. This is the core of the gospel: the atonement for sin, the payment of debt and the earning of forgiveness by Jesus on our behalf. Paul will build his argument on this basis later in the epistle.

   o This sacrifice is what makes possible our salvation. It delivers us from an evil world system of sin, condemnation and death. Before Christ came, the world was in darkness and ignorant of God's will.

o   This was all done according to the will and purpose of God. All of human history worked towards this (I Timothy 2:4).

^{5} to whom be the glory forevermore. Amen.

Man was created in order to give glory to God; this is the basic meaning to his life. In giving God glory and honor man finds peace, joy, a sense of purpose and eternal life.

Paul recognizes this fact and reaffirms it in his greeting and also in his assessment of the things done by God for man, through Jesus Christ. God deserves glory for what He has done, and receives the glory He is due through the countless number of saints who glorify Him because of, and through, Jesus.

The word "Amen" comes from a Hebrew word which meant surely, to be firm, steady or trustworthy. It is pronounced "Aw-mane" in Hebrew, and was translated into Greek, Latin and English (just as "baptism" was transliterated from the Greek word "baptizo"). The literal translation into English means "verily" or "truly." It was used as a responsive formula with which the Jewish listener acknowledged the validity of an oath or curse, and willingness to accept its consequences (Numbers 5:22; Deuteronomy 27:15).

Jesus used the term to confirm that what He was about to say was sure, trustworthy and without doubt.

Verily, verily I say to you, the hour is coming…
- John 5:25

The New Testament uses the word as an agreement with an offering of praise or a blessing. It was also used in synagogue worship in this way, and as Jews were converted the saying of Amen at the end of praise, blessings, prayers and teaching passed into the Christian worship.

13

Paul uses it in this way at the end of his greeting, confirming that it is a sure and trustworthy thing that:

1. Jesus died for sins — Amen
2. Was resurrected — Amen
3. This was according to God's will — Amen
4. God deserves glory for all of this — Amen

The Jews in the Old Testament used it to confirm oaths and receive prophecy. Jesus used it to underscore His words and prophecy. The Apostles used it in their writings in words of blessings, praise and teachings. The early church used it to signal their approval of what was being preached and emphasize their faith in what was being taught. To say Amen in church is a biblical, respectful and encouraging way to demonstrate agreement and enthusiasm for what is being prayed about, taught, preached and sung in church. We should do more of it.

2.
THE DANGERS
OF FALSE TEACHING

Paul is writing to the churches in the Roman province of Galatia concerning the false teaching being spread among them. To become Christian, one first had to become a Jew (e.g. circumcision); this was being taught by a group (Judaizers) within the church.

The danger of this teaching was that:

1. It added to the gospel by requiring additional responsibilities from the believer beyond a confession of faith, repentance and baptism. It added to the word spoken by Jesus.

2. By accepting circumcision the person was in affect saying that he was abandoning salvation through union with Christ based on faith and now would pursue salvation based on the perfect keeping of the Law.

3. The danger here was that salvation by faith in Christ was and continues to be possible for man, but salvation by law keeping was impossible for man (man is unable to accomplish law keeping sufficiently to achieve perfection, Romans 3:23).

In the first verse, Paul establishes his authority as an Apostle, and reminds them of the core of the gospel:

1. The debt for sin was fully paid by Jesus.

   o Restitution was made by Jesus, we have nothing to give.

   o Repentance, a change of attitude toward God and sinfulness, is made by man.

2. This plan was from God and he deserves glory for devising it.

Once having done this, Paul goes on to immediately chastise them for moving away from this central teaching.

Accusation

> [6] I am amazed that you are so quickly deserting Him who called you by the grace of Christ, for a different gospel;

Paul marvels at the speed with which they are turning away from God. The gospel comes from God and to turn away from it is to turn away from God Himself. Paul is amazed that this thing is happening so quickly after their conversion. It's an early stage in their faith, a critical time, and they are already having problems. They are in the process of turning away from God. Their turn is not complete yet, but dangerously close.

God calls all to be saved, and the gospel is the tool that He uses to call men and women to it. The gospel contains the message of the death, burial and resurrection of Christ as well as the necessary response of faith in repentance and baptism. The grace of Christ can better be translated as "God called you graciously through Christ." It is through the gracious work of Christ and the proclamation of it that men are called by God.

The Galatians had quickly abandoned the spirit and conditions of this call for what they thought was a superior gospel, and Paul marvels at this.

> [7] which is really not another; only there are some who are disturbing you and want to distort the gospel of Christ.

In reference to the "gospel" brought to them by the Judaizers, Paul makes the following statements:

- The Judaizers were promoting their teachings as the true or superior gospel and claiming that Paul was not teaching them accurately.

- Paul responds that there was no such thing as "another gospel" because there was only one gospel.

- The resulting confusion was that the original gospel was being changed into something else that did not resemble or achieve what the original gospel achieved.

- Paul described the true motives behind the false teachers' actions:

  o They wanted to unbalance and disturb the Galatians in their faith.

  o They were doing this to suit their own prejudices (they wanted to be saved by law-keeping and wanted others to follow suit).

These people preached about Christ and claimed to be from God, but they were false because what they preached was different than what Christ had preached. Even today this holds true—if what you teach about salvation is false, you are a "false teacher."

The Warning

Paul quickly issues a warning directed at these Judaizers and anyone else who would distort (change, add or subtract) the gospel.

> [8] But even if we, or an angel from heaven, should preach to you a gospel contrary to what we have preached to you, he is to be accursed!

Everyone who preaches a different gospel originally preached by Paul and the Apostles stands condemned by God. This includes Apostles or anyone claiming authority, even Paul or angels (visions, dreams, etc.). This does not include devils because they are already condemned. Angels are the most powerful beings next to God, but even they will be condemned if they change the gospel. Condemned, not because Paul orders the church to pronounce this curse on those who distort the gospel, but condemned because Jesus has already condemned those who do this (Matthew 23:13-39).

> [9] As we have said before, so I say again now, if any man is preaching to you a gospel contrary to what you received, he is to be accursed!

Paul repeats the injunction including any person (includes Pharisees who are not spirits and who have no Apostolic authority) who distorts the gospel. Paul repeats that this is not a new warning, he has said it before.

The Judaizers were deserving of the curse because:

- They knew the gospel and believed it (Acts 15:5).

- They were now knowingly changing it despite the warnings and the letter sent by the Apostles concerning this matter (Acts 15:1-77).

- They were encouraging others to follow their example in this heresy (Galatians 1:7).

Paul rebukes them for being unfaithful to the gospel in such little time, establishing that there is only one true gospel (that was originally preached by himself and the other Apostles) and condemns anyone who changes it.

Basic Lessons

1. There is only one gospel.

Jesus gave the Apostles the ministry of proclaiming that all must obey it to be saved (Matthew 28:20). The contents of it were never to change (1 Corinthians 15:1-5). The church was to resist any attempt to add, subtract or change it (Jude 3).

In the Galatian letter we see that the first attack against the church was an attack not against the people, but against the message (not that it was not true, merely an attempt to adjust it).

2. Judge the messenger by the message.

Many messengers claim to be from God: superior intelligence, visions, secret knowledge, etc., but the true test of credibility is the accuracy of the message. Reputation, education or speaking style do not make up for a false message.

Beware of the majority of messengers' traps. The gospel is written so all can understand. It will be true even if the whole world falls into error. Stick with the message, no matter what.

3. False gospels do not save.

In I Timothy 4:16, Paul says that in continuing to preach the truth, Timothy would ensure salvation for himself and the church. The opposite is also true, to fall away from the true message is to lose salvation.

The urgency with which Paul writes to the Galatians is necessary because in turning away from grace to law for salvation, they were turning from salvation to damnation. Those who preach a false gospel will be damned and those who follow it will also be damned; one through rebellion and distortion, the others through ignorance and foolishness.

Examples of false gospels are those that teach that:

- o Jesus is not the Son of God.

- o Jesus has not resurrected.

- o We need to add or subtract from faith, repentance and baptism in order to be saved.

These will not save the learner and will condemn the teacher. We need to guard our doctrine and our church against false teachers.

3.
CHRONOLOGY OF PAUL'S EARLY LIFE

The letter to the Galatians is an appeal by Paul to churches in the Roman province of Galatia to resist the movement to abandon the system of salvation that saves one by faith in Christ (expressed in repentance and baptism), and adopt a system of salvation whereby one is justified by the keeping of the Law (expressed in circumcision, ritual and food law).

The Judaizers were Jewish Christians, formerly Pharisees, who taught that salvation by the keeping of the Law in Jesus' name was the superior way and they were seducing non-Jewish Christians into believing this idea.

Paul is amazed that the Galatians are so quickly moved by this false teaching. He dismissed it as false and rebukes the teachers for having spread it.

The Judaizers claimed special status and tried to discredit Paul as an Apostle. In response, Paul describes his early life and contacts with Peter in order to establish his own credibility and relationship with Peter the Apostle whom the Judaizers accepted and respected.

Outline

In our outline we see Paul mentioning three meetings with Peter. These occur over a period of more than fifteen years. The meetings he mentions in Galatians are:

His first meeting with Peter alone to share his conversion experience when he returns to Jerusalem for the first time after becoming a Christian (Galatians 1:10-17).

The second meeting is during the Jerusalem conference to discuss the question of the "Circumcision Party" and a letter is written and sent by Paul to the churches (Galatians 2:1-10).

The third meeting occurs in Antioch when Paul challenges Peter for his hypocrisy in withdrawing his association with the Gentiles for fear of the Circumcision Party (which he condemned in Jerusalem before) (Galatians 2:11-14).

Today, I would like to fit these three meetings into the larger picture of Paul's life and try to reconstruct the events in order of appearance.

Chronology

There is no orderly chronology of Paul's life in the New Testament. We have to piece together his life from different scriptures and matching historical data from the period.

1. Birth

> But Paul said, "I am a Jew of Tarsus in Cilicia, a citizen of no insignificant city; and I beg you, allow me to speak to the people."
> - Acts 21:39

Tribe of Benjamin (Philippians 3:3); Judah and Benjamin were the only two tribes in the southern kingdom. Because of their help to the Roman army, the citizens of the province of Celicia were all granted Roman citizenship. This was a right usually purchased by military people or slaves. It carried advantages of movement, freedom and special protection under Roman law.

This occurred approximately 100 years before Paul was born. This, then, is how Paul, a Jew, could at the same time claim Roman citizenship merely by mentioning the place of his birth. Paul was probably a little younger than Jesus.

2. Training

> "I am a Jew, born in Tarsus of Cilicia, but brought up in this city, educated under Gamaliel, strictly according to the law of our fathers, being zealous for God just as you all are today.
> - Acts 22:3

He came to Jerusalem at a young age and was educated and trained by Gamaliel. Gamaliel was the grandson of Hillel, a rabbi who held the more lenient view over divorce (School of Shammai was the other). He was a member of the Sanhedrin and argued in favor of the Apostles before the Sanhedrin (Acts 5:33). He was held in such high favor by the Jews that they conferred on him the title of "Rabban" which means our teacher, a higher title than "Rabbi" which means my teacher.

Paul rose in influence himself, having been taught by such a man.

He is the one holding the coats (perhaps in official capacity) when Stephen is stoned to death (Acts 7:54).

Saul begins to persecute the church following the death of Stephen (Acts 9:1-2). He wanted to return to the area which he came from to persecute the church and bring Christians back to Jerusalem for trial and punishment.

3. Conversion

[3] As he was traveling, it happened that he was approaching Damascus, and suddenly a light from heaven flashed around him; [4] and he fell to the ground and heard a voice saying to him, "Saul, Saul, why are you persecuting Me?" [5] And he said, "Who are You, Lord?" And He said, "I am Jesus whom you are persecuting, [6] but get up and enter the city, and it will be told you what you must do." [7] The men who traveled with him stood speechless, hearing the voice but seeing no one. [8] Saul got up from the ground, and though his eyes were open, he could see nothing; and leading him by the hand, they brought him into Damascus. [9] And he was three days without sight, and neither ate nor drank.

[10] Now there was a disciple at Damascus named Ananias; and the Lord said to him in a vision, "Ananias." And he said, "Here I am, Lord." [11] And the Lord said to him, "Get up and go to the street called Straight, and inquire at the house of Judas for a man from Tarsus named Saul, for he is praying, [12] and he has seen in a vision a man named Ananias come in and lay his hands on him, so that he might regain his sight." [13] But Ananias answered, "Lord, I have heard from many about this man, how much harm he did to Your saints at Jerusalem; [14] and here he has authority from the chief priests to bind all who call on Your name." [15] But the Lord said to him, "Go, for he is a chosen instrument of Mine, to bear My name before the

Gentiles and kings and the sons of Israel; [16] for I will show him how much he must suffer for My name's sake." [17] So Ananias departed and entered the house, and after laying his hands on him said, "Brother Saul, the Lord Jesus, who appeared to you on the road by which you were coming, has sent me so that you may regain your sight and be filled with the Holy Spirit." [18] And immediately there fell from his eyes something like scales, and he regained his sight, and he got up and was baptized;

[19] And I said, 'Lord, they themselves understand that in one synagogue after another I used to imprison and beat those who believed in You.
- Acts 9:3-18; 22:19

Note that he heard Jesus' voice. He was blinded and then regained his sight. He learned through prophecy what the Lord was calling him to (preach to the Gentiles). Nevertheless was baptized on order to wash away his sins.

Some say that we, in the churches of Christ, focus too much attention on baptism, but Ananias insisted on it for Paul.

4. Escape from Damascus

[19] Now for several days he was with the disciples who were at Damascus, [20] and immediately he began to proclaim Jesus in the synagogues, saying, "He is the Son of God." [21] All those hearing him continued to be amazed, and were saying, "Is this not he who in Jerusalem destroyed those who called on this name, and who had come here for the purpose of bringing them bound before the chief priests?" [22] But Saul kept increasing in

> strength and confounding the Jews who lived at Damascus by proving that this Jesus is the Christ.
>
> [23] When many days had elapsed, the Jews plotted together to do away with him, [24] but their plot became known to Saul. They were also watching the gates day and night so that they might put him to death; [25] but his disciples took him by night and let him down through an opening in the wall, lowering him in a large basket. - Acts 9:19-25

King Aretas (II Corinthians 11:32) who ruled the region during this time, dies in 40 AD and so we know approximately the time Paul was converted.

5. Arabia

> [17a] nor did I go up to Jerusalem to those who were apostles before me; but I went away to Arabia,

Desert region. Went there to meditate, pray, to be taught and also for safety's sake for he was a hunted man.

6. Return to Damascus

> [17b] and returned once more to Damascus.

7. First meeting with Peter in Jerusalem

> [18] Then three years later I went up to Jerusalem to become acquainted with Cephas, and stayed with him fifteen days.

Three years after his conversion, he spent two weeks in Jerusalem. He met only with Peter and James to share his experiences but not to receive instructions from them.

After meeting with Peter he spent some time preaching in the area and debated with Hellenists (Jews reared among Greeks in other lands, Greeks who had converted to Judaism). It was the same group with whom Stephen originally debated and who brought him before the Sanhedrin (Stephen was also a Hellenist converted to Christianity). The ones he had plotted with before, he now debates with concerning Christ. These Hellenists begin to plot to murder Saul in the same way, and so he is brought out of the city in Cesarea and then back to Tarsus.

8. Syria and Cilicia

[21] Then I went into the regions of Syria and Cilicia.

Paul remains in this area for about ten years. He preached in Tarsus. II Corinthians 11:22-27 talks about several things not mentioned in Acts that some believe may have happened during his time in Syria

[22] Are they Hebrews? So am I. Are they Israelites? So am I. Are they descendants of Abraham? So am I. [23] Are they servants of Christ? —I speak as if insane—I more so; in far more labors, in far more imprisonments, beaten times without number, often in danger of death. [24] Five times I received from the Jews thirty-nine lashes. [25] Three times I was beaten with rods, once I was stoned, three times I was shipwrecked, a night and a day I have spent in the deep. [26] I have been on frequent journeys, in dangers from rivers, dangers from robbers, dangers from my countrymen, dangers from the Gentiles, dangers in the city, dangers in the

wilderness, dangers on the sea, dangers among false brethren; [27] I have been in labor and hardship, through many sleepless nights, in hunger and thirst, often without food, in cold and exposure.

Period of maturing and preparation for his great work among the Gentiles is largely done here.

9. Paul brought to Antioch by Barnabas

[19] So then those who were scattered because of the persecution that occurred in connection with Stephen made their way to Phoenicia and Cyprus and Antioch, speaking the word to no one except to Jews alone. [20] But there were some of them, men of Cyprus and Cyrene, who came to Antioch and began speaking to the Greeks also, preaching the Lord Jesus. [21] And the hand of the Lord was with them, and a large number who believed turned to the Lord. [22] The news about them reached the ears of the church at Jerusalem, and they sent Barnabas off to Antioch. [23] Then when he arrived and witnessed the grace of God, he rejoiced and began to encourage them all with resolute heart to remain true to the Lord; [24] for he was a good man, and full of the Holy Spirit and of faith. And considerable numbers were brought to the Lord. [25] And he left for Tarsus to look for Saul; - Acts 11:19-25

Gentiles receive Christ in the area and Apostles send Barnabas to work with this group. Barnabas goes to Tarsus and gets Paul to work with him. Paul is used to working with people in that area and culture, Barnabas serves as his mentor.

10. Relief trip for Jerusalem church

> [27] Now at this time some prophets came down from Jerusalem to Antioch. [28] One of them named Agabus stood up and began to indicate by the Spirit that there would certainly be a great famine all over the world. And this took place in the reign of Claudius. [29] And in the proportion that any of the disciples had means, each of them determined to send a contribution for the relief of the brethren living in Judea. [30] And this they did, sending it in charge of Barnabas and Saul to the elders.
> - Acts 11:27-30

Time of persecution, Peter is in hiding (Acts 12:6-17).

11. Return to Antioch

> [25] And Barnabas and Saul returned from Jerusalem when they had fulfilled their mission, taking along with them John, who was also called Mark.
> - Acts 12:25

Bring John Mark back with them from Jerusalem.

12. First missionary

> [1] Now there were at Antioch, in the church that was there, prophets and teachers: Barnabas, and Simeon who was called Niger, and Lucius of Cyrene, and Manaen who had been brought up with Herod the tetrarch, and Saul.
> - Acts 13:1

Churches in Galatia are established. Approximately thirteen years after his conversion. God calls, God prepares, God sends.

13. Second meeting with Peter

[1] Then after an interval of fourteen years I went up again to Jerusalem with Barnabas, taking Titus along also. [2] It was because of a revelation that I went up; and I submitted to them the gospel which I preach among the Gentiles, but I did so in private to those who were of reputation, for fear that I might be running, or had run, in vain. [3] But not even Titus, who was with me, though he was a Greek, was compelled to be circumcised. [4] But it was because of the false brethren secretly brought in, who had sneaked in to spy out our liberty which we have in Christ Jesus, in order to bring us into bondage. [5] But we did not yield in subjection to them for even an hour, so that the truth of the gospel would remain with you. [6] But from those who were of high reputation (what they were makes no difference to me; God shows no partiality)—well, those who were of reputation contributed nothing to me. [7] But on the contrary, seeing that I had been entrusted with the gospel to the uncircumcised, just as Peter had been to the circumcised [8] (for He who effectually worked for Peter in his apostleship to the circumcised effectually worked for me also to the Gentiles), [9] and recognizing the grace that had been given to me, James and Cephas and John, who were reputed to be pillars, gave to me and Barnabas the right hand of fellowship, so that we might go to the Gentiles and they to the circumcised. [10] They only asked us to remember the poor—the very thing I

also was eager to do.
- Galatians 2:1-10

Fourteen years after his original two week visit in Jerusalem with Peter, he returns again to share the results of his work with the church, including Peter.

This was the occasion of the meeting talked about in Acts 15, when the Apostles sent a letter out concerning the Judaizers.

14. Third meeting with Peter

[11] But when Cephas came to Antioch, I opposed him to his face, because he stood condemned. [12] For prior to the coming of certain men from James, he used to eat with the Gentiles; but when they came, he began to withdraw and hold himself aloof, fearing the party of the circumcision. [13] The rest of the Jews joined him in hypocrisy, with the result that even Barnabas was carried away by their hypocrisy. [14] But when I saw that they were not straightforward about the truth of the gospel, I said to Cephas in the presence of all, "If you, being a Jew, live like the Gentiles and not like the Jews, how is it that you compel the Gentiles to live like Jews?
- Galatians 2:11-14

Paul returns to Antioch and some time later Peter visits and this is the conflict over Peter's hypocrisy concerning the Gentiles and the Judaizers.

15. Second missionary journey

> [36] After some days Paul said to Barnabas, "Let us return and visit the brethren in every city in which we proclaimed the word of the Lord, and see how they are."
> - Acts 15:36

> [22] When he had landed at Caesarea, he went up and greeted the church, and went down to Antioch.
> - Acts 18:22

16. Third missionary journey – Acts 18:23-21:16

> [23] And having spent some time there, he left and passed successively through the Galatian region and Phrygia, strengthening all the disciples.

> [16] Some of the disciples from Caesarea also came with us, taking us to Mnason of Cyprus, a disciple of long standing with whom we were to lodge.

17. Paul's first imprisonment in Rome (61-63 AD) – Acts 21:17-28:31

> [17] After we arrived in Jerusalem, the brethren received us gladly.

> [31] preaching the kingdom of God and teaching concerning the Lord Jesus Christ with all openness, unhindered.

He was arrested in Jerusalem and sent to Rome for his hearing before Ceasare. Was then eventually released.

18. Brief freedom and final work with the church (64-66 AD)

> [5] For this reason I left you in Crete, that you would set in order what remains and appoint elders in every city as I directed you, [6] namely, if any man is above reproach, the husband of one wife, having children who believe, not accused of dissipation or rebellion.   - Titus 1:5-6

After his release he visited Crete with Titus and later writes to him to complete the work they had began there together (65 AD).

During this period Paul did not go to Spain as he had hoped to do when writing to the Roman church years before (Romans 15:28). Instead he chose to revisit churches that he had previously established or encouraged:

- Crete – Titus 1:5
- Ephesus – I Timothy 1:3
- Corinth – II Timothy 4:20
- Miletus – II Timothy 4:20
- Troas – II Timothy 4:13

19. Second imprisonment and death

> [6] For I am already being poured out as a drink offering, and the time of my departure has come.
> - II Timothy 4:6

Historians record that the emperor, Nero, was responsible for starting the fire that destroyed the city of Rome in 64 AD

(Tacitus – a roman historian eventually converted). He wanted an excuse to rebuild the city and played the fiddle in enjoyment while it burned. In order to divert blame from himself, he accused Christians of setting fire to the city because they considered it an unmoral place.

It was during the following years of persecution that Paul, as a visible Christian leader, was re-arrested and eventually beheaded in 66-67 AD (he died before the destruction of Jerusalem in 70 AD).

4.
HOW PAUL OBTAINED THE GOSPEL

Paul is rebuking those who are teaching a gospel different than the gospel he and the other Apostles originally delivered to the Galatians. They taught that the true gospel included not only faith in Jesus Christ and baptism as an expression of that faith, but also full adherence to the Jewish Law and custom fully accepted in circumcision.

They accused Paul of toning down the demands of the "true gospel" (which included circumcision) in order to gain favor with Gentiles, to make the gospel palatable to them. Their argument was that in his zeal and ambition to build churches among the Gentiles, Paul had stripped the gospel of some of its teachings (i.e. circumcision). They said that these teachings were in accordance with what was taught in Jerusalem.

The Judaizers came to Galatia in order to restore it to its true content. Their plan was to first discredit Paul and then to substitute what they taught for what Paul had originally taught. Their plan was succeeding and so Paul writes this urgent letter denouncing the Judaizers and re-confirming the fact that the gospel he gave them was the only true gospel and that anyone who taught anything else should be cursed.

This background explains why he says in Galatians 1:10 that he is not trying to please men, and his language concerning the Judaizers in this letter was not the kind of language used to please men, but he was speaking as a servant of Christ.

> [10] For am I now seeking the favor of men, or of God? Or am I striving to please men? If I were still trying to please men, I would not be a bond-servant of Christ.

Paul responds to accusations that his gospel is not the same as the other Apostles with three replies:

1. The fact that he received the gospel from Christ Himself and not second-hand from other Apostles.

2. That the other Apostles fully acknowledge Paul's gospel.

3. That on one occasion he was obliged to correct Peter himself regarding this very point of liberty from the Law, and that Peter accepted the correction.

As far as the Galatians and Judaizers were concerned, if Paul and Peter argued on the substance of the gospel, that settled it. All replies tied into his meetings with Peter.

Paul begins by explaining that the gospel he preached to them was originally received by him from Jesus Himself and later confirmed by Peter, Jesus's chosen Apostle, at their first meeting in Jerusalem.

> [11] For I would have you know, brethren, that the gospel which was preached by me is not according to man. [12] For I neither received it from man, nor was I taught it, but I received it through a revelation of Jesus Christ.
> - Galatians 1:11-12

Paul refers to the gospel (the content and response) that he originally preached to them was not taught to him by man, but came to him as a revelation from God:

1. He knew about Jesus because he was a Jew in Jerusalem.

2. He met Jesus in a miraculous way on the road to Damascus.

3. He obeyed Jesus just like everyone else, by being baptized.

4. He received the ability to know and teach accurately all the things that Christ taught in the same way the Apostles did, through the power of the Holy Spirit given to him by Christ (John 16:13).

> [13] For you have heard of my former manner of life in Judaism, how I used to persecute the church of God beyond measure and tried to destroy it; [14] and I was advancing in Judaism beyond many of my contemporaries among my countrymen, being more extremely zealous for my ancestral traditions.

Paul explains his own conversion. He persecuted the church and did so "beyond measure," he was fanatical about it, extremist, not only wanting to limit its growth but wanting to destroy it.

The reason for his fanaticism is that he was raised to be a strict Pharisee, zealous for tradition. The Rabbis had created a series of six hundred and thirteen human commandments, which they built around the Law as a hedge, to protect the purity of the Law. The Pharisees were the "guardians" of these human commandments or traditions. For example, the Law said no work on the Sabbath. The Rabbis created a number of rules to protect this command such as the prohibition to walk more than a certain distance, or the prohibition of a scribe to carry his pen. The Pharisees were then to teach and enforce these laws.

Paul, the zealous Pharisee, was so against Christianity because the church meant death to Phariseeism. Paul saw the crown of Judaism in the traditions that he fought to preserve and knew that if Jews became Christians they might keep parts of the Mosaic Law (adultery, murder, stealing, etc.) that were confirmed by Jesus, but quickly do away with the burdensome traditions from which Christianity had freed them.

The Judaizers were merely Jewish Pharisees who had become Christians, and who wanted to impose these things on Christianity in the same way they were imposed on Judaism. Their starting point was circumcision, but they would have certainly added from there in the same way they had added to the Law in the Old Testament.

Paul reminds them that he was the worst of these Pharisees, but now he preached freedom from these things in Christ. Why? Because of the revelation received from Christ, since no man could have convinced him. If anyone should have been a Judaizer he was the perfect candidate, but he was against it because it was against the gospel.

> [15] But when God, who had set me apart even from my mother's womb and called me through His grace, was pleased [16] to reveal His Son in me so that I might preach Him among the Gentiles, I did not immediately consult with flesh and blood, [17] nor did I go up to Jerusalem to those who were apostles before me; but I went away to Arabia, and returned once more to Damascus.

Paul refers to both his conversion and commission in the same context.

1. God knew from the very beginning of Paul's life that when he was called, he would respond.

2. It was the grace of God expressed in the death of Jesus for sin that Paul responded to, this is what melted his heart.

3. God's purpose for him was to demonstrate the living Christ in the dramatically changed life of Paul. What better way than through the transformed life of a fanatical Jew who formerly despised Gentiles?

Paul says that when this transformation happened to him, he did not consult with other Apostles first, but went off to Arabia and then returned to Damascus for some time.

> [18] Then three years later I went up to Jerusalem to become acquainted with Cephas, and stayed with him fifteen days. [19] But I did not see any other of the apostles except James, the Lord's brother. [20] (Now in what I am writing to you, I assure you before God that I am not lying.)

Only after three years did he go to Jerusalem and meet with Peter and James for two weeks. No repudiation or rejection came from them, and if he were not genuine he would have been revealed as a false Apostle at this time.

> [21] Then I went into the regions of Syria and Cilicia. [22] I was still unknown by sight to the churches of Judea which were in Christ; [23] but only, they kept hearing, "He who once persecuted us is now preaching the faith which he once tried to destroy." [24] And they were glorifying God because of me.

On the contrary, he went into the northern regions of Syria and Cilicia to preach and other places kept hearing of his success in preaching the gospel in these areas. Note that all were glorifying God because of his ministry. There was no disapproval by the Apostles, and this is his point. From the beginning his gospel has not been rejected but rather encouraged by Peter and the other Apostles. So his first reply to their accusations is to refer to the divine source of his gospel.

All the Apostles acknowledge the contents of his gospel – 2:1-10

During the interval between his time in Syria we know that Paul:

1. Was brought to Antioch by Barnabas to teach.

2. Gathered funds for a relief mission concerning Jerusalem.

3. Returned with Barnabas and John Mark to Antioch.

4. Went on his first missionary journey and established the churches in Galatia.

The Judaizers begin to cause trouble in these and other churches with their false doctrine and attacks against Paul. These events go by in a period of fourteen years, and now Paul finds himself back in Jerusalem with all the Apostles and the church this time.

Paul is describing in Galatians 2:1-10 what Luke also describes in Acts 15:

1. Paul has returned from his first missionary journey and is reporting in Antioch the things they have done.

2. The Judaizers begin to debate with them there and so the church sends them down to Jerusalem to get the opinion of the Apostles there.

3. Paul, Barnabas, Titus and others go down to Jerusalem.

4. They reported this work to the church and the Judaizers challenged them openly again.

5. The Apostles and elders gathered together with Paul, Barnabas and the Judaizers to explain the matter.

6. The outcome was that the Apostles and elders supported Paul and confirmed his gospel and work, and wrote a letter to all the churches proclaiming this, thus repudiating the Judaizers and their doctrine.

Paul is now commenting on the events in Galatians 2:1-10 as he tells the story to the Galatians.

> [1]Then after an interval of fourteen years I went up again to Jerusalem with Barnabas, taking Titus along also. [2] It was because of a revelation that I went up; and I submitted to them the gospel which I preach among the Gentiles, but I did so in private to those who were of reputation, for fear that I might be running, or had run, in vain.

Paul is guided by the Lord to go and lay his cares before the other Apostles. The fear raised by the Judaizers in the minds of the Galatians was that all of Paul's work had been for nothing (running in vain) because his gospel was not true, but Paul was laying it before the Apostles themselves to show it was not for nothing.

> [3] But not even Titus, who was with me, though he was a Greek, was compelled to be circumcised.

He quickly demonstrates that his work was not in vain since Titus, a Greek, was not required to be circumcised even by the Apostles in Jerusalem. Positive proof that the Judaizers' claims were groundless.

> [4] But it was because of the false brethren secretly brought in, who had sneaked in to spy out our liberty which we have in Christ Jesus, in order to bring us into bondage. [5] But we did not yield in subjection to them for even an hour, so that the truth of the gospel would remain with you.

He did this (report to the Apostles) because of the challenge of the Judaizers, who want to restrict their freedom in Christ. They were false brethren. Their purpose was to imprison the brothers with the Law again. Paul did not give in to their demands so that they might remain free in Christ (this demand was that Titus be circumcised as a test case for their position – Paul refused and stood his ground because if Titus was not circumcised in Jerusalem, none in Galatia would be either).

In verses 6-10 Paul summarizes the outcome of the confrontation with the Judaizers and meeting with the Apostles and leaders in Jerusalem.

> [6] But from those who were of high reputation (what they were makes no difference to me; God shows no partiality)—well, those who were of reputation contributed nothing to me.

Those who were reported to be of high reputation in comparison to me by the Judaizers, did not object to, add or subtract from the gospel that is presented.

Paul considers himself and the other Apostles as equal in the Lord's service; it was the Judaizers who tried to elevate one against the other. In God's sight, God makes no partiality between brethren based on name, reputation or position. The Apostles did not do this, Paul did not do this, but the Judaizers tried.

> [7] But on the contrary, seeing that I had been entrusted with the gospel to the uncircumcised, just as Peter had been to the circumcised [8] (for He who effectually worked for Peter in his apostleship to the circumcised effectually worked for me also to the Gentiles), [9] and recognizing the grace that had been given to me, James and Cephas and John, who were reputed to be pillars, gave to me and Barnabas the right hand of fellowship, so that we might go to the Gentiles and they to the circumcised.

Peter, James and John gave Paul and Barnabas the right hand of fellowship as a public witness of their solidarity of purpose, and content of message (what we do when someone joins our fellowship). They recognized that Paul's Apostleship and gospel had the same source as their own. Paul's ministry to the Gentiles was encouraged and confirmed, as was this to the Jews.

> [10] They only asked us to remember the poor—the very thing I also was eager to do.

They even argued to share the work among the poor within the churches.

In this way, Paul demonstrates how his ministry and his message was confirmed by all the Apostles and how the false gospel of the Judaizers had been rejected by the Apostles in Jerusalem.

Lessons

It is not who you know, who you are, how educated or not you are; it is what you preach and teach that is important. God can raise up preachers from any race or social position and put the zeal of ministry into his heart. This is why, in looking for ministers, the most important qualifications we seek are knowledge of, faithfulness to, and zeal for God's word.

We cannot grow as a church if we are more involved in arguing over the word than proclaiming it to the lost. We need to stay focused on spreading the gospel and teaching what we know and are sure of, rather than wasting time and energy debating and dividing over issues that don't affect our souls. Jesus said, "Go into all the world and preach the gospel to all creation." (Mark 16:15), not, "Go and debate the brethren at all the lectureships."

5.
SAVED BY FAITH

So far in our study of Galatians we have seen that Paul is defending himself against accusations that he has changed the gospel in order to make it more palatable to Gentiles by removing certain commands concerning circumcision. His accusers, the Judaizers, were charging that they and the "true" Apostles, like Peter in Jerusalem, were teaching the original gospel which included circumcision and law keeping.

In describing his past associations with Peter and the other Apostles, Paul demonstrates that they have always been supportive and in agreement with the gospel he preached, not the one promoted by the Judaizers.

In Galatians 2:11-21 Paul goes even further to recount a time when even Peter himself was untrue to the gospel and Paul had to correct him in defense of the pure message of salvation in Jesus.

Peter's Rebuke – 2:11-14

> [11] But when Cephas came to Antioch, I opposed him to his face, because he stood condemned.

Paul establishes the place and seriousness of the problem. Because of his error in judgment on the matter of the gospel, Peter stood condemned. In an incident that he will describe later, Paul says that he opposed Peter publicly. (There is no basis in the Bible for apostolic and subsequent papal infallibility.)

> ^{12} For prior to the coming of certain men from
> James, he used to eat with the Gentiles; but when
> they came, he began to withdraw and hold himself
> aloof, fearing the party of the circumcision.

Peter visited Antioch, a Jewish/Gentile church to which this letter was sent from the Jerusalem meeting. While there he mingled and ate with Gentiles, which Christians were free to do, but unconverted Jews were not.

"Certain men from James" probably means Jewish Christians from Jerusalem, associates of James, who also came to Antioch. Peter was afraid that they might report to the church in Jerusalem that he was associating with Gentiles in Antioch, and when the Judaizers learned this they would cause problems for Peter when he returned. Peter's reaction was to withdraw from the Gentiles and not mingle or eat with them anymore.

> ^{13} The rest of the Jews joined him in hypocrisy, with
> the result that even Barnabas was carried away by
> their hypocrisy.

Peter's actions prompted other Jewish Christians to do the same, even Barnabas (who helped Paul establish churches among the Gentiles in Galatia).

This was very dangerous because:

- It gave power to the Judaizers in promoting false gospel.

- It built up a wall between Jew and Gentile in the church, a wall that Christ had taken down.

- A respected leader takes the first steps back into legalism and draws others with him.

54

> ¹⁴ But when I saw that they were not straightforward about the truth of the gospel, I said to Cephas in the presence of all, "If you, being a Jew, live like the Gentiles and not like the Jews, how is it that you compel the Gentiles to live like Jews?

Paul confronts Peter publicly about his hypocrisy. Peter was condemning what he himself practiced because of the fear of criticism. Peter was neither bound by law nor the traditions being promoted by the Judaizers, but by his separation from the Gentiles he was supporting the idea that the Gentiles should be.

Paul's Argument – 2:15-21

Paul reviews the basis of the argument that he had made to Peter and the rest of the church at Antioch during that confrontation.

> ¹⁵ "We *are* Jews by nature and not sinners from among the Gentiles; ¹⁶ nevertheless knowing that a man is not justified by the works of the Law but through faith in Christ Jesus, even we have believed in Christ Jesus, so that we may be justified by faith in Christ and not by the works of the Law; since by the works of the Law no flesh will be justified

Paul begins by explaining that even the Jews, who were the chosen people of God (unlike the Gentiles who were in total darkness), recognized that salvation was obtained through Christ and not through law.

What was the ideological conflict between Paul and the Judaizers concerning the Law? Paul believed and taught that the true purpose of the Law (commandments and ordinances) was to reveal sin and how God dealt with sin (Romans 3:20). The giving of the Law was not an end unto itself, but rather a step in God's overall plan to save man. Here is where the Law fit in:

- God created man righteous (good and acceptable).

- Man sinned and became unrighteous and this unrighteousness made him subject to God's judgment and condemnation.

- God planned to save man from this condemnation, but before this could happen God had to bring man to a certain point in understanding:

    - He had to bring man to the knowledge of the true God since after his fall into sin, man was easily seduced into the worship of false gods (idolatry).

    - God also needed to teach man the nature of sin and how it affected his life.

    - It was also necessary to reveal to man how God was going to save him from the sure condemnation and punishment for sin he faced at judgment.

- God began this process of education slowly by first revealing Himself to a few men (Noah, Abraham, Isaac, Jacob, etc.) and then to the whole Jewish nation through Moses.

- Next, He began to reveal to man the reason and result of his condition.

This is where the Law came in. It was given to reveal what sin was, its impact on mankind and how God was going to deal with it (the sacrificial system pointing to eventual atonement by the Messiah).

Once man had learned from the Law that sin causes spiritual blindness and death, and that God deals with sin through the method of atonement (the payment of one life for another), he was prepared to recognize two things:

1. He was a sinner and it was his own sin that condemned him.

2. The final sacrifice for sin was the perfect life of Jesus, the Savior sent by God.

The righteousness that man had at creation in Adam was recreated again in Jesus, and just as all shared in Adam's fallen nature, all could now share in the righteousness of Christ through union with Him by faith. We are connected to Adam by flesh, and therefore share in his sin. However, we are also connected to Jesus by faith and thus share in his perfection.

Paul taught that man was saved because he shared in the righteousness of Christ through faith, and the Law served to reveal man's unrighteousness and the way Jesus dealt with it through his atoning death on the cross.

When the Pharisees spoke of the Law, they included all of the man made traditions that had grown up around the Law. In many instances they used a perverted view of the Law to establish their own righteousness. They did not see the Law as something to reveal sin, but rather as something to conquer sin. They claimed that they were righteous in God's eyes for two reasons: they were the chosen people of God, and they actually obeyed the Law.

The problem with this self-view was that they were chosen to be the people through whom Christ would come in order to deal with sin, but they were not just chosen arbitrarily as the saved people. They obeyed their version of the Law, but Jesus showed how shallow their concept of the Law really was. For example, in their interpretation of the Law, adultery was defined as sex with the legitimate wife of a fellow Jew, not a single woman, widow, slave, or divorcing without cause. Jesus, in the Sermon on the Mount, demonstrated just how demanding the Law really was when it came to adultery. He said that simply lusting in your heart for a woman, any woman, was adultery.

The Judaizers, who were Pharisees that had become Christians, wanted to introduce a system whereby man could achieve righteousness by obeying certain laws, like circumcision or certain food restrictions. Paul maintained that in living a perfect life and offering it on the cross, Jesus obeyed the entire law. Christians, in turn, became obedient to that law not by keeping every command, but by being united to Jesus by faith. Both Paul and the Judaizers had the same objective: to be perfect and thus be saved. Their method required obeying all the commands one by one until perfect. Paul, on the other hand, taught that God's method for being perfect was to share in Jesus' perfection by faith.

> [17] But if, while seeking to be justified in Christ, we ourselves have also been found sinners, is Christ then a minister of sin? May it never be!

In defending this way Paul asks the question, "Do we sin by trying to be justified through faith rather than through law?" In the end, this is what the Judaizers are saying. If this is so, he says, we make Christ to be the one who leads us into sin because He is the one who says to believe in Him. Heaven forbid!

> [18] For if I rebuild what I have once destroyed, I prove myself to be a transgressor.

If he reestablishes the system of salvation by works of law that he removed when accepting Christ, two things automatically happen:

1. He will be condemned by the very laws he is reestablishing. The system of law can only reveal and condemn but it cannot make someone perfect, which is what is necessary to be saved.

2. Christ will condemn Paul for abandoning the true way of salvation: faith in Him.

Either way, he will become a transgressor.

> [19] For through the Law I died to the Law, so that I might live to God.

Paul declares that when he understood the true purpose of the Law (to reveal sin, etc.) and recognized his true sinfulness and condemnation under the Law, he stopped trying to use the Law as a means of saving himself (he died to the Law). He did this so he could be saved by Christ (live to God).

This imagery of him "dying to the Law" and "living to God" is a wonderful parallel to what he says in the next verse where he repeats the same idea, but now uses different imagery. This time his death is on the cross and his life is the resurrected one with Christ.

> [20] I have been crucified with Christ; and it is no longer I who live, but Christ lives in me; and the life which I now live in the flesh I live by faith in the Son of God, who loved me and gave Himself up for me.

The old Paul, who depended on the works of the Law for righteousness and salvation, died with Christ, a death expressed and experienced in baptism (Romans 6:3).

The new Paul, righteous, perfect and saved, has Christ's presence within himself through the actual indwelling of the Holy Spirit (Acts 2:38).

You die in baptism and you resurrect from baptism with Christ in you through the Holy Spirit.

Everything now done with his flesh is no longer done to earn righteousness through law keeping. Paul's behavior is now a response of trusting faith in a savior who loved and died in his place in order to confer upon Paul the perfection necessary to be acceptable in God's eyes and thus saved. Previous acts done as works of law were burdens, discouraging and produced a false sense of pride. Now, the very same things done as a response of faith are acceptable to God, joyful to do and create humility in the believer's heart.

> [21] I do not nullify the grace of God, for if righteousness comes through the Law, then Christ died needlessly."

Paul is not the one eliminating the grace of God; Peter and the Judaizers are doing this by returning to the old system. Paul argues that If righteousness could be obtained in this way, Christ would have died for nothing. God did not send Him to die for some sins. Jesus was sent to die for all sins. His death pays for all sin, or no sin. It is one or the other: You either accept perfection through union with Christ based on faith, or you pursue it through perfect law keeping.

It is one or the other. You cannot have both. The problem in the Galatian church and in many churches since is that people try to mix the two systems and end up with various forms of legalism as a result.

Paul mentions nothing more of Peter here or elsewhere, so we assume that Peter received the correction, adjusted his position and his later letters seem to confirm this.

6.
THE SPIRIT AND POWER COME THROUGH FAITH

In his letter to the Galatians, Paul is reviewing the core ideas and benefits of the gospel message that he originally preached to them. He also warns them against the distorted gospel brought to them by the Judaizers.

It is interesting to note that both Paul and the Judaizers had the same objective, it was their methods that were different. The Judaizers wanted to be perfect and thus be saved from condemnation and hell. Their method to achieve this was to obey the commands of the Law of Moses (beginning with circumcision) and receive salvation as a reward. Paul recognized that the way to salvation was to be sin free. He argued that the way to this perfection was to receive it as a gift from God based on one's faith in Jesus Christ.

The thrust of Paul's argument was that in living an absolutely perfect and sinless life, Jesus fulfilled all the demands of the Law. In offering His perfect life on the cross, He paid the moral debt owed to God for all sinners. Those who believed in Him received freely the same perfection that He had earned by living a perfect life.

This perfection, this absolute obedience, Paul calls righteousness. Righteousness by faith is perfection granted by virtue of one's union to Christ by faith in Him (which he later explains is expressed in repentance and baptism). This is why there is salvation in no other person but Jesus. Not because God is cruel and will not accept sincere offers of worship from other religions who have ancient and reverent worship practices. There is no salvation outside Jesus because only Jesus fulfills the requirements of the Law that is universal in its demands and condemnation. Only in Jesus can one be considered perfect and thus spared the condemnation that will come from the final judgment of God. The only access to perfection is through Jesus. That is why there is no salvation outside of Him since there is no other way to be perfect before God.

Why are faith and baptism so important then? Because it is the point where one is united to Jesus in order to be saved. This was God's way of making man perfect and no other way was to be substituted. Here are a few reasons why:

- God decreed that it would be so. Righteousness was to be by faith, not law (Galatians 3:11). God's word is what brings a principle or a thing into being and gives it legitimacy. Therefore, there is no relationship between faith and moral excellency unless God says so.

- Righteousness is a gift and cannot be earned. Man began righteous, he was created this way, it was a gift to him at creation. The new man becomes righteous again as a gift from God when he is recreated in Christ (Romans 3:23-34; 6:23).

- Righteousness by faith glorifies God and puts man solely at His mercy and into proper submission (Romans 3:27-28). God subdues His enemies with wrath and destruction (II Thessalonians 1:7-8). God brings His children into submission through grace and the offer of righteousness by faith (I Corinthians 1:26-31). Either way, we will submit to Him.

In Galatians 2:15-21, Paul establishes the idea that this righteousness is obtained through faith. Jesus' faith was expressed in perfect obedience to the Father (what we cannot do), and the believer's faith expressed in repentance and baptism (what we can do). It is because we believe in Jesus that we are united to Him and it is because we are united to Him that we are perfect according to the Law.

Now Paul goes on to describe other things that are obtained through faith, which cannot be obtained through the keeping of the Law.

Paul demonstrates that not only righteousness is obtained by faith but other spiritual blessings as well, such as the regenerative work of the Holy Spirit within them. He shows this by asking five questions to the Galatians, starting in chapter 3:

> [1] You foolish Galatians, who has bewitched you,
> before whose eyes Jesus Christ was publicly
> portrayed as crucified?

Paul asks, **"What is the matter with you?"** They are being foolish and thoughtless in what they are doing, that is, abandoning perfection through faith to try to obtain it by perfect law keeping. How can they even think of doing this after Christ has been so plainly and publicly presented to them through Paul's teaching? The fact that Christ earned everything for them through His cross was so plainly stated and portrayed, how could they be so foolish as to discard this? Who is fooling them?

> [2] This is the only thing I want to find out from you:
> did you receive the Spirit by the works of the Law,
> or by hearing with faith?

How did they receive the Holy Spirit? They were mostly Gentiles with no previous knowledge of the Law. When they heard Paul's preaching they responded with faith and received the Holy Spirit (Acts 2:38). If it was not received by faith, how then did they receive the Holy Spirit?

> [3] Are you so foolish? Having begun by the Spirit, are you now being perfected by the flesh?

What system is working in you now? With the Spirit also came the regenerative power in their lives as they began bearing the fruit of the Christian character. They knew that this change was begun by the Holy Spirit who was received by faith. Are they now trying to complete the work of the Holy Spirit through human efforts bound to the Law? How can what was begun by the Spirit without the help of human effort be completed by human effort?

> [4] Did you suffer so many things in vain—if indeed it was in vain?

Was it all for nothing? They suffered for this faith through various persecutions. Paul asks if all of it was for nothing now that they are threatening to throw it all away. "If indeed it was in vain" is another way of saying that Paul cannot bring himself to believe so until it happens. He still has hope for them.

> [5] So then, does He who provides you with the Spirit and works miracles among you, do it by the works of the Law, or by hearing with faith?

Where do the miracles come from? God had done signs among them through Paul when he preached to them. God had given them the Holy Spirit at the preaching of Paul. How was this done? Was it done based on their response of faith or works of law? The Judaizers did no miracles while among them to confirm their gospel, but the true Apostles with the true gospel were confirmed by miracles and signs just as Jesus said they would be (Mark 16:20).

Summary

Paul re-establishes that the blessings of salvation were obtained by Jesus because He obeyed the Law perfectly and offered His life for sin. Those who want to receive these blessing do so by being united to Christ by faith and thus share in the blessings he has obtained.

So far, Paul has mentioned two of the blessings of salvation: righteousness and the Holy Spirit, and both are received freely as one is united to Jesus by faith, not by keeping the Law. Paul reminds the Galatians how they originally received these blessings to prevent them from throwing them away.

Practical Lesson

In closing out this chapter I'd like to answer a common question that often comes up when discussing this issue of righteousness obtained by faith:

"If I am already perfect in God's eyes, why do I struggle to avoid disobedience, why do I make efforts to do good works?"

Both Judaizers and Paul struggled against sin and made human efforts to do good, the difference was why they did it. The Judaizers did it in order to be perfect and thus earn salvation. Paul said that whatever good he did was prompted by the Spirit within him and carried out as an act of faith to glorify God, because God had already saved him through Christ.

The Christian does what he does to glorify God and lift up Christ, and his faith that saves him is evident in this. Those who make no effort to serve God, deny sin, and refuse to confess Christ demonstrate that they have no faith and thus are separated from Jesus and salvation.

7.
BLESSINGS AND FAITH

Paul's key point thus far in his letter to the Galatians is that the blessings of salvation are obtained through a system of faith, not law. He argues that it is our association with Jesus based on our faith in Him that enables us to share in the many blessings that accompany salvation He brings. One could compare it to a poor person marrying someone who is rich. You share in the wealth by marriage, not by merit. In this example, baptism would be the wedding ceremony where the poor person (the sinner) is united with the one who is rich (Christ).

In the previous chapter we began discussing some of the blessings that are obtained by faith and how to keep these in our possession. Paul has mentioned two so far: the blessing of righteousness and the blessing of the Holy Spirit dwelling in us. These are obtained by faith, not works of law and tradition as the Judaizers claimed.

Paul also mentions that we maintain these blessings in the same way that we obtain them: by faith. I continue to be righteous before God because I continue to believe in Jesus, not because I manage to get everything right after I become a Christian.

In citing these two blessings Paul speaks to both Jews and Gentiles. In chapter 3:6 however, he mentions another blessing received by faith that his Jewish readers would identify with more than their Gentile brethren. This was the promise of Abraham, another blessing received exclusively through faith in Christ. In verses 6-29 Paul not only explains that the promise of Abraham comes through faith in Christ, but that the Gentiles receive it in the very same way.

Before getting into the text, let us first review what Paul is referring to when he mentions the promise of Abraham. When God originally made this promise He was assuring that Abraham would receive:

1. Protection from his enemies.

2. A great nation that would descend from him.

3. A land of his own.

4. Blessings for himself and that all nations would be blessed through him.

With time these promises were summarized by Jesus as being the assurance that they were God's special children, that their land would always be theirs and they would always be protected by God.

Paul will go on to explain that the essence of the promise was that Abraham and his descendants were being blessed and preserved so that through them Jesus would ultimately come and when he did, all of the spiritual blessings promised would be given to Him, to Jesus!

Once Christ had obtained all of the blessings then everyone would have access to them through a system of faith. This was God's plan in distributing the spiritual blessings of heaven as promised to Abraham.

Blessings Have Always Been Based on Faith

> ⁶ Even so Abraham believed God, and it was reckoned to him as righteousness. ⁷ Therefore, be sure that it is those who are of faith who are sons of Abraham.

Paul begins by demonstrating that the faith system has always been the principle by which God operated. Even with Abraham, God imparted righteousness based on his faith. He was not inventing a new system but rather fulfilling the system which had always been in place. Sons of Abraham were all those who arrived at righteousness in the same way Abraham did: through a system of faith.

> ⁸ The Scripture, foreseeing that God would justify the Gentiles by faith, preached the gospel beforehand to Abraham, saying, "All the nations will be blessed in you." ⁹ So then those who are of faith are blessed with Abraham, the believer.

The heart of the gospel message, the good news, is not that Jesus is Lord; the good news is that through Jesus the Lord salvation is offered to man based on faith (otherwise he could not obtain it).

As the first one to hear and believe the message Abraham would:

1. Himself be blessed with righteousness.

2. Be the spiritual father of all those who would respond in the same way. In this manner all nations would have access to the blessings of salvation because they would be offered through a system of faith.

Paul brushes aside the Judaizers' argument (that one must first be circumcised and follow Jewish customs and laws before becoming a disciple of Jesus) by saying that only through his gospel could one truly become a "son of Abraham."

> [10] For as many as are of the works of the Law are under a curse; for it is written, "Cursed is everyone who does not abide by all things written in the book of the Law, to perform them." [11] Now that no one is justified by the Law before God is evident; for, "The righteous man shall live by faith." [12] However, the Law is not of faith; on the contrary, "He who practices them shall live by them." [13] Christ redeemed us from the curse of the Law, having become a curse for us—for it is written, "Cursed is everyone who hangs on a tree"—[14] in order that in Christ Jesus the blessing of Abraham might come to the Gentiles, so that we would receive the promise of the Spirit through faith.

Now Paul contrasts the system of salvation by law keeping

Verse 10: Law was given to reveal sin and condemn sinners. Anyone trying to justify themselves through law keeping had to perform perfectly. There was no grace, and any failure led to condemnation.

Verses 11-12: Paul argued that Scripture itself (the Law and the prophets) taught that righteousness came through the faith system, not the Law keeping system. The gospel he preached therefore did not violate Jewish theology.

Verse 13: That the Savior was crucified was an obstacle to faith for the Jewish mindset. Jesus' death and especially the manner of it did not fit the image of a glorious savior that they expected and also seemed to violate the Scriptures concerning someone who was executed.

Paul goes on to explain that the curse of the Law was that everyone's sins were revealed by the Law and consequently were condemned by that same law. And yet even with this knowledge men were helpless to stop sinning or remove the punishment that hung over them. The Law did not give one the power to stop sinning or provide any way to appeal to God for mercy or forgiveness. Those were its main weaknesses. Jesus came and annulled this curse in three ways:

1. He lived a perfect life and thus fulfilled the requirements of the Law once and for all.

2. He offered His life in order to pay the moral debt owed by all men on account of sin. This was done according to the demands of the Law. A perfect life to redeem an imperfect life, and since His was a divine as well as a human nature, the quality of His sacrifice was such that it could pay for the sins of all men not just one man.

3. He promised to give the Holy Spirit to all men so that they would be empowered to stop sinning.

Paul explains Christ's death was the curse He bore for us. It was a shameful thing for a Jew to die on a tree (executed as a criminal), but Paul says that it was our shame, our deserved curse that He innocently bore for us. The Apostle explains the curse in relationship to Christ's work on the cross in order to help Jews see that the curse was shameful indeed, but it was our shame that Christ bore, not His own.

Verse 14: Once the curse had been removed, everyone could now be blessed. The Jews had access to righteousness because the Law that condemned them had been fulfilled. The Gentiles had access to righteousness because the Law that had limited them had been removed.

75

> ^{15} Brethren, I speak in terms of human relations: even though it is only a man's covenant, yet when it has been ratified, no one sets it aside or adds conditions to it.

After establishing the idea that salvation through a system of faith has always been God's way of dealing with man, Paul begins a new thought.

He explains a principle of law familiar to them:

- That when a covenant (testament) is made and ratified, you cannot undo it or change it afterwards (like a will).

- This cannot be done with man-made laws and certainly not with God's laws either.

> ^{16} Now the promises were spoken to Abraham and to his seed. He does not say, "And to seeds," as referring to many, but rather to one, "And to your seed," that is, Christ.

In the next verse Paul makes his point. The promise or covenant was made by God with Abraham. This covenant was established. The basis of the promise was that the seed of Abraham would receive the promised blessings (Genesis 22:18). He explains that the seed of Abraham was Jesus Christ. The blessings were not intended for the Jews alone as a special nation, but rather for Jesus Christ who would come out of this nation.

> ^{17} What I am saying is this: the Law, which came four hundred and thirty years later, does not invalidate a covenant previously ratified by God, so as to nullify the promise.

Four centuries after Abraham, Moses led the people out of Egypt, and God gave Moses the Law. The point is that this giving of the Law did not change the original covenant made with Abraham. Christ was still to be the recipient of the blessings and the faith system the manner in which all would have access to them. The Law did not change this.

> [18] For if the inheritance is based on law, it is no longer based on a promise; but God has granted it to Abraham by means of a promise.

The blessings were originally promised and received by faith, but if the system was changed and now they are obtained by law keeping, two things happen:

1. You have added and changed God's original covenant.

2. There are no longer any gifts based on promise, they must now be earned.

> [19] Why the Law then? It was added because of transgressions, having been ordained through angels by the agency of a mediator, until the seed would come to whom the promise had been made.

Now Paul answers a natural question that might be posed to him at this juncture, "Why was the Law given?" In answering this question he explains that God gave the Law by the hand of angels through the mediator, Moses, for several reasons:

1. For transgressions

   o   To reveal sin

   o   To mitigate against evil (divorce, food, etc.)

   o   To reveal condemnation on account of sin

2. To prepare men for Christ (the seed)

- o To reveal God's way of dealing with sin through atonement and the sacrificial system. Atonement for sin requires death.

[20] Now a mediator is not for one party only; whereas God is only one.

The Law did not replace the promise or change the promise in any way, and the way it was given demonstrates this. The promise was given directly by God to Abraham, one on one, as a covenant is done. The Law was given to the people by a mediator, Moses, who received it from God amid thousands of angels (Deuteronomy 33:2). The Law was not an addition to or a limitation of the promise, but rather a divinely appointed and temporary measure whose purpose was served when Christ came.

[21]Is the Law then contrary to the promises of God? May it never be! For if a law had been given which was able to impart life, then righteousness would indeed have been based on law. [22]But the Scripture has shut up everyone under sin, so that the promise by faith in Jesus Christ might be given to those who believe.

Even though the Law does not change the original promise to Abraham or cancel it, Paul is quick to add that it does not contradict or work against the purpose of God either. Paul merely points out what it was not meant to do, and that was to make men righteous. It was brought in to prepare men to understand their own sinfulness and how God was to deal with it through Christ, and then offer righteousness through a system of faith as originally promised to Abraham. First the promise, then the Law to prepare men for the promise, then the fulfillment of the promise in Christ.

After explaining that the faith system is scriptural, and then providing the reason and purpose of the Law, Paul summarizes how both worked together to bring us to Christ and the end result of this.

> [23] But before faith came, we were kept in custody under the Law, being shut up to the faith which was later to be revealed. [24] Therefore the Law has become our tutor to lead us to Christ, so that we may be justified by faith. [25] But now that faith has come, we are no longer under a tutor.

Paul uses the word faith in two different ways: faith as belief, and faith as in the faith, the gospel, the revelation of promise.

Verse 23: Before Jesus came, the Law served as a restrainer, to guide or mitigate until the gospel was revealed.

Verse 24: Tutors were usually well-educated slaves who were responsible for the care and education of rich young Roman and Greek boys. They were not the parents but had the necessary authority from the parents to discipline and train the child. Once the child came to maturity he was then released from the tutor, free to receive his inheritance.

Paul makes this analogy in reference to the Law and how it trained and disciplined God's people until they were ready for sonship, maturity and the inheritance promised from their Father. God used the Law to prepare us to receive the promises by faith in Jesus Christ.

Verse 25: Now that the faith (Gospel) has come, it is the sign that the tutor (the Law) is no longer necessary. It has served its purpose.

> [26] For you are all sons of God through faith in Christ Jesus. [27] For all of you who were baptized into Christ have clothed yourselves with Christ. [28]

79

> There is neither Jew nor Greek, there is neither slave nor free man, there is neither male nor female; for you are all one in Christ Jesus. [29] And if you belong to Christ, then you are Abraham's descendants, heirs according to promise.

Verse 26: The principle summarized. The essence of the promise was that all would become sons of God and inherit the blessings that come with that position. That promise is obtained through the faith system originally revealed to Abraham. The gospel reveals the one who demonstrated perfect faith, obtained all the blessings for us and in whom our faith must be: Jesus.

Verse 27: The expression of faith is explained. Abraham expressed his faith beginning with circumcision and ending with the offer of his own son Isaac. He wasn't perfect and failed in many ways, but his intention was to remain faithful. Our expression of faith begins with baptism and ends with offering of ourselves as living sacrifices in service and purity (Romans 12:1-2).

According to the Bible, faith has three components: trust, obedience and acknowledgement. Many have an incomplete definition of biblical faith seeing it merely as an acknowledgement of the proposition that Jesus is the Son of God without the elements of trust or obedience.

Abraham's faith is the model:

1. He trusted God to provide for him.

2. He acknowledged God's presence.

3. He obeyed God's directive, with the intention to obey perfectly. (This is why only God can judge, because only He can see the effort of the heart.) He did not

always do this well, but the purpose of his will was to do it and thus he was considered righteous.

Verse 28: The result of the faith system. Unity of believers through Jesus Christ. Men are still men and women are still women, but now through this system of faith they can all have a relationship with God and with one another on a spiritual level that was not possible before. This does not free slaves, give women authority in the church or eliminate cultural differences—we are still what we are and still play the roles we do. What it does do, however, is reveal that in God's eyes all those united to Christ are of equal value and recipients of the blessings.

Verse 29: The purpose of God's plan. God fulfills His original promise to Abraham: all nations are blessed through the seed of Abraham—Jesus Christ. For the Jews who knew the scriptures, the revelation was not that the Gentiles would be saved (this was repeated often by the prophets); the great revelation was that they, the Jews, would be united to the Gentiles in order to form one people in Christ.

Summary

In this long passage Paul has one objective and deals with three issues. His objective is to show that the promise made to Abraham (in all of its terms: sonship, righteousness, blessings, etc.) was obtained through a system of faith, in the same way that all the other spiritual blessings are apprehended. The faith system has always been the way God has transferred blessings to man. In this context he explains three things:

1. The faith system is scriptural; it was what God required of Abraham and of everyone who was to come to Him, both Jew and Gentile.

2. He explains the scope and purpose of the Law. Why God gave it and what it could and could not do.

- o It could prepare us for Christ.
- o It could not change God's faith system.
- o It could not make men righteous.

3. He summarizes how the Law worked to bring us to Christ and the result of the faith system. The faith system produced:

- o Personal righteousness.
- o Unity in Christ for all regardless of culture, sex or class.

8.
FREEDOM THROUGH FAITH

From chapter 2:15 until the end of chapter 4 Paul is teaching on one particular theme: the way that spiritual blessings are transferred from God to man.

Some in the church (Pharisees and Circumcision Party) were beginning to teach that God gave the blessings in exchange for obedience to the Law, and circumcision was the sign that one held to this; Christ was now the new "law giver."

Paul defended the idea that blessings were transferred on the basis of faith. All blessings were earned by Christ and all those who were united to, or had a relationship with Christ by faith shared in the blessing that He possessed. Baptism was the initial expression of this faith. This was Paul's main point here, and he goes on to demonstrate how each individual blessing (righteousness, spirit, power and sonship) was meant for us through Christ by faith.

In the final section Paul describes the last of these blessings: freedom. He will explain how this gift, like all the others, is obtained by Christ and available to all through the faith system.

Sonship Comes by Faith – 4:1-7

> [1] Now I say, as long as the heir is a child, he does not differ at all from a slave although he is owner of everything, [2] but he is under guardians and managers until the date set by the father. [3] So also we, while we were children, were held in bondage under the elemental things of the world. [4] But when the fullness of the time came, God sent forth His Son, born of a woman, born under the Law, [5] so that He might redeem those who were under the Law, that we might receive the adoption as sons. [6] Because you are sons, God has sent forth the Spirit of His Son into our hearts, crying, "Abba! Father!" [7] Therefore you are no longer a slave, but a son; and if a son, then an heir through God.

In the previous section Paul has explained how the true sons of Abraham are those who receive the blessings as Abraham did, through faith and not through keeping of law.

The opening section of chapter four has two purposes:

1. To summarize the transformation spoken of before, from slave to son.

2. To provide a bridge to the next large section dealing with the idea of freedom.

This is how Paul writes: he explains a point and then creates a bridge idea in order to summarize his thoughts and prepare the reader for the next idea he will present.

These two ideas do not follow one after another, but rather are mingled together in these verses.

> [1] Now I say, as long as the heir is a child, he does not differ at all from a slave although he is owner of

everything, [2]but he is under guardians and managers until the date set by the father. [3]So also we, while we were children, were held in bondage under the elemental things of the world.

Paul reviews the idea of guardians that a son is placed under. He highlights that even though the son is to inherit all, he is no better than a slave while under the tutor. The "elemental things" are the ABC's of knowledge:

- The physical applications and restrictions of the Law regarding food, sacrifice, social customs, etc.

- God's sons should live above these kinds of things, but until Christ, were subject to them instead.

[4] But when the fullness of the time came, God sent forth His Son, born of a woman, born under the Law, [5] so that He might redeem those who were under the Law, that we might receive the adoption as sons.

Jesus came in the flesh to suffer and submit Himself to all the same restrictions so He could offer the perfect sacrifice of Himself, and thus pay the debt caused by the Law thereby freeing man from the bondage/tutorage of the Law. It is as if Jesus learned and performed all the lessons required by tutor so we could have freedom from the tutor. He writes our final exam and passes it with 100%.

[6] Because you are sons, God has sent forth the Spirit of His Son into our hearts, crying, "Abba! Father!" [7] Therefore you are no longer a slave, but a son; and if a son, then an heir through God.

Once Christ has accomplished the removal of the tutor and brought us into sonship, we are prepared to receive the inheritance of sons of God: the Holy Spirit who brings us into mature intimacy with our Father. Paul repeats that one who has this relationship with God through the Spirit made possible by Christ is no longer a slave, but rather a son.

In the next section Paul will continue this line of thinking, but will discuss the issue in the light of freedom rather than sonship.

Return to Bondage – 4:8-11

> [8]However at that time, when you did not know God, you were slaves to those which by nature are no gods. [9]But now that you have come to know God, or rather to be known by God, how is it that you turn back again to the weak and worthless elemental things, to which you desire to be enslaved all over again? [10]You observe days and months and seasons and years. [11]I fear for you, that perhaps I have labored over you in vain.

Having established how they obtained their sonship and thus their freedom, he admonishes them for abandoning this precious gift and returning to bondage and slavery.

Verse 8: He reminds the Gentiles of Galatia, that although the Jews were slaves kept under the Law, they (the Gentiles) were slaves to idols, which was worse. The Law was preparing the Jews for Christ, the Gentile idols led to nothing.

Verses 9-11: Paul rebukes them for desiring to return to the type of enslavement (basic things) that characterized both Jewish and Gentile past. He is afraid his work may have been for nothing.

Appeal of Love – 4:12-20

[12] I beg of you, brethren, become as I am, for I also have become as you are. You have done me no wrong; [13] but you know that it was because of a bodily illness that I preached the gospel to you the first time; [14] and that which was a trial to you in my bodily condition you did not despise or loathe, but you received me as an angel of God, as Christ Jesus Himself. [15] Where then is that sense of blessing you had? For I bear you witness that, if possible, you would have plucked out your eyes and given them to me. [16] So have I become your enemy by telling you the truth? [17] They eagerly seek you, not commendably, but they wish to shut you out so that you will seek them. [18] But it is good always to be eagerly sought in a commendable manner, and not only when I am present with you. [19] My children, with whom I am again in labor until Christ is formed in you— [20] but I could wish to be present with you now and to change my tone, for I am perplexed about you.

Paul makes an emotional appeal for them to remember how enthusiastically they received him when he first came to them and to return to that type of relationship and position.

Verse 12: Paul, the Jew under law, became like them (the Gentiles without the Law) when he became a Christian. Now, they are becoming like he used to be (under law) and he says they should become like he is now (not under law). He holds no grudge against them, it is not his honor that is at stake—it is their souls!

Verses 13-15: In the beginning they received him with enthusiasm, even though he was sick when he originally came. "Plucking out eyes" was an expression like "giving the shirt off your back."

Verses 16-18: Paul asks if they are rejecting him because he is telling them the truth, a truth that they do not want to hear at the moment. The Judaizers are pressuring them in an unjust manner so that the Galatians will honor them, and are doing it by establishing themselves as the only teachers that the Galatians will listen to. Paul says it is good to be sought after as a teacher but for the right reasons, and not only when he is among them in person. He was sought by them when there, but they have strayed in his absence.

Verses 19-20: He uses the tender language of an expectant parent who suffers as a child (who she nourishes with her own body) is fully formed. He wishes he could be there in person to convey by the tone of his voice what he desires for them because he is at his wit's end with concern for their well-being.

Allegory of Sarah and Hagar – 4:21-31

21 Tell me, you who want to be under law, do you not listen to the Law? 22 For it is written that Abraham had two sons, one by the bondwoman and one by the free woman. 23 But the son by the bondwoman was born according to the flesh, and the son by the free woman through the promise. 24 This is allegorically speaking, for these women are two covenants: one proceeding from Mount Sinai bearing children who are to be slaves; she is Hagar. 25 Now this Hagar is Mount Sinai in Arabia and corresponds to the present Jerusalem, for she is in slavery with her children. 26 But the Jerusalem above is free; she is our mother. 27 For it is written,

"Rejoice, barren woman who does not bear; Break forth and shout, you who are not in labor; For more numerous are the children of the desolate Than of the one who has a husband."

> ²⁸ And you brethren, like Isaac, are children of promise. ²⁹ But as at that time he who was born according to the flesh persecuted him who was born according to the Spirit, so it is now also. ³⁰ But what does the Scripture say?
>
> "Cast out the bondwoman and her son, For the son of the bondwoman shall not be an heir with the son of the free woman."
>
> ³¹ So then, brethren, we are not children of a bondwoman, but of the free woman.

An allegory is a term that refers to a story that has a superficial and a deeper meaning. Paul tells the Galatians that the story of Sarah and Hagar is an allegory with a superficial and a deeper meaning that is pertinent to their situation.

Verse 21: He now resumes his argument from his emotional appeal of a few verses before. Those who claim that what they do is according to the Law do so in ignorance of what the Law is really saying. He proceeds to reveal the deeper significance of the story told within the pages of the Law.

Verses 22-23: Abraham was promised a son by Sarah. When he did not arrive, Sarah gave him her slave, Hagar, to conceive. Hagar conceived Ishmael but was put out of the house by Sarah once Sarah conceived Isaac, the child of promise. The implication is that the child that came by the promise has preeminence over the natural son.

Verses 24-27: Paul explains the deeper meaning of this story: Hagar represents the Law, Sarah represents grace.

Hagar represents the present Jerusalem, under Judaism, without Christ, under bondage to the Law, coming from

Mount Sinai in Arabia where the Law was given and thus outside the land of promise.

Sarah represents the Jerusalem from above, God's grace in fulfillment of his promise to her. Those who belong to the spiritual Jerusalem do so because of God's grace and promise in Christ, not because of nationality or law. Isaiah 54:1 reinforces the idea that the descendants of Sarah (desolate) would ultimately be greater than the one who gave birth naturally (Hagar).

Verses 28-31: Like Isaac, Christians are children of the promise, not law (and they receive the promise through faith).

It is not surprising, then, that the Judaizers (who are in a sense the descendants of the bondwoman, Hagar, whose son Ishmael persecuted Isaac, the son of promise) should persecute Christians (sons of the free woman, Sarah) in the same way.

In Genesis we know that Sarah cast out Hagar and her son when this happened. Paul says that in the same way they should cast out any attempt to displace them as well as any doctrine or person that tries to rid them of their position as free men and sons of promise. He repeats this in verse 31.

Lessons

1. From the very beginning God promised that the spiritual blessings of righteousness, Holy Spirit, sonship and freedom would be given through His son Jesus Christ. There is no other religion or philosophy mentioned.

2. These blessings were available to all who would be united to Christ by faith (expressed through repentance and baptism).

3. The Law was introduced in history in order to mitigate the evil of sin and prepare man for the coming of Christ. It did not have the power to confer any blessings.

4. Anyone who attempted to gain these blessings through some form of law keeping would fail, anyone who taught this should be rejected and would ultimately be cursed.

9.
A CALL TO LIVE
IN FREEDOM

The book of Galatians was originally written as an effort to turn a church away from its fall into legalism. In Romans 9:30-33 Paul explains the basic error of legalism:

> [30]What shall we say then? That Gentiles, who did not pursue righteousness, attained righteousness, even the righteousness which is by faith; [31] but Israel, pursuing a law of righteousness, did not arrive at that law. [32] Why? Because they did not pursue it by faith, but as though it were by works. They stumbled over the stumbling stone, [33] just as it is written,
>
> "Behold, I lay in Zion a stone of stumbling and a rock of offense,
> And he who believes in Him will not be disappointed."

Gentiles, even religious ones, did not pursue holiness and purity as the Jews did and captured the blessings, but the Jews did not. Why? The Jews were pursuing the Law which is in itself righteous, but did not and could not impart righteousness. The Gentiles captured the righteousness that saves because they pursued it from the starting point of faith (in Christ). The Jews lost the righteousness that saves because they rejected Christ as the starting point and chose to try to capture or possess righteousness by capturing the Law instead. This involved doing and becoming right by obeying the Law perfectly.

The Gentiles were united to Christ by faith (trust and obedience expressed in repentance and baptism) and so gained the blessings of salvation earned for them by Jesus. The Jews tried to unite themselves to the Law (through perfect obedience) hoping that the qualities that the Law possessed would then be theirs.

The Judaizers wanted the Galatians to attempt to gain righteousness through union with the Law and express that in circumcision. In chapters 5 and 6 Paul makes a final plea for them to reject this system and remain firmly united to Christ by faith.

Reject Circumcision – 5:1-12

[1] It was for freedom that Christ set us free;
therefore keep standing firm and do not be subject again to a yoke of slavery.

[2] Behold I, Paul, say to you that if you receive circumcision, Christ will be of no benefit to you. [3] And I testify again to every man who receives circumcision, that he is under obligation to keep the whole Law. [4] You have been severed from Christ, you who are seeking to be justified by law; you have fallen from grace.

Paul exhorts them to remain united to Christ telling them that to unite themselves to the Law through circumcision will effectively sever them from Christ. They cannot have it both ways. If you accept circumcision, you accept everything that the Law prescribes.

Christ gives the blessings of salvation freely, but those seeking these from the Law must pay the price of perfect obedience to gain them (which is impossible).

> [5] For we through the Spirit, by faith, are waiting for the hope of righteousness. [6] For in Christ Jesus neither circumcision nor uncircumcision means anything, but faith working through love.

Those united to Christ by faith have a true hope of righteousness and their "works" are not to obtain righteousness, but rather expressions of love motivated by faith.

Therein lies the essential difference between these two systems:

- Legalism produces good works, a moral lifestyle and a pious attitude, but the motivation is pride! God will give me righteousness because of the good that I do.

- Faith produces exactly the same results, except the motivation is gratitude for mercy received in dealing with one's sins. Faith motivates by love for God because He first loved us.

- Legalism fails because it cannot produce a loving heart, the very image of God.

> [7] You were running well; who hindered you from obeying the truth? [8] This persuasion did not come from Him who calls you. [9] A little leaven leavens the whole lump of dough. [10] I have confidence in you in the Lord that you will adopt no other view; but the one who is disturbing you will bear his

> judgment, whoever he is. [11] But I, brethren, if I still preach circumcision, why am I still persecuted? Then the stumbling block of the cross has been abolished. [12] I wish that those who are troubling you would even mutilate themselves.

This is an exhortation to not abandon faith for legalism, and a reproach on those who would lead them in this direction and a reminder that this did not come from himself.

Verses 7-10: He wonders who led them astray after such a good start and voices an opinion suggesting that he believes that they will not abandon the faith. This legalism is not of Christ, and those who promote it work among them like leaven. This is obliviously a warning to be careful. He also makes a warning to the one who is advocating this view that God will judge him for this.

Verses 11-12: We see the suggestion that Paul was also preaching circumcision and the Apostle responds to this here:

- If he does, why is he still persecuted by the Judaizers?

- If he does, then what purpose is the cross? If by an act of merit we can be accepted by God, why the cross? Either Jesus earns it all or nothing.

Paul suggests that if the Judaizers really want to outdo him (which is what they were trying to do, to show their religious zeal as superior to his), he says they should go all the way and castrate themselves! Perhaps this would impress the Galatians on their zeal and sincerity.

True Walk of Freedom – 5:13-6:10

In verse 1 Paul equates union with Christ with freedom. He goes on to say that righteousness, the Holy Spirit, power and sonship all come to us based on our union with Christ as does freedom.

In the next verses he explains that Christian freedom does not mean license to be immoral. Freedom and maturity bring additional responsibility and accountability. Paul explains what freedom in Christ really means.

Service

> [13] For you were called to freedom, brethren; only do not turn your freedom into an opportunity for the flesh, but through love serve one another. [14] For the whole Law is fulfilled in one word, in the statement, "You shall love your neighbor as yourself." [15] But if you bite and devour one another, take care that you are not consumed by one another.

We are united to the One who came on earth to serve, not to be served. We are free to serve others in the name of the Lord and reap the rewards of satisfaction, joy and peace that come from service. We were originally created to serve and that is our most natural and fulfilling activity. Before we served sin, self and the devil; now we are free to serve God, others and the kingdom. All service (in and out of the kingdom) done in Jesus' name is holy. Any service offered without regard to Christ will perish with this earth.

Fruitfulness

> [16] But I say, walk by the Spirit, and you will not carry out the desire of the flesh. [17] For the flesh sets its desire against the Spirit, and the Spirit against the flesh; for these are in opposition to one another, so that you may not do the things that you please. [18] But if you are led by the Spirit, you are not under the Law. [19] Now the deeds of the flesh are evident, which are: immorality, impurity, sensuality, [20] idolatry, sorcery, enmities, strife, jealousy, outbursts of anger, disputes, dissensions, factions, [21] envying, drunkenness, carousing, and things like these, of which I forewarn you, just as I have forewarned you, that those who practice such things will not inherit the kingdom of God. [22] But the fruit of the Spirit is love, joy, peace, patience, kindness, goodness, faithfulness, [23] gentleness, self-control; against such things there is no law. [24] Now those who belong to Christ Jesus have crucified the flesh with its passions and desires.
>
> [25] If we live by the Spirit, let us also walk by the Spirit. [26] Let us not become boastful, challenging one another, envying one another.

Freedom means that we are able to bear the kind of spiritual fruit that will last forever because we are no longer separated from God or cursed to be destroyed along with everything else we've built or tried to preserve, whether good or bad. The key is to walk after the Spirit (obey the word) and in so doing we will bear the everlasting marks of the Holy Spirit.

The works of the Holy Spirit are evident in a person's character and cannot be denied. If you bear the works of the flesh more consistently than the fruit of the Spirit, it is obvious that you don't walk after the Spirit and will not inherit the kingdom.

We are free to follow the Spirit as Christians. Christ has given us His spirit, but we are capable of rejecting Him if we want to and whether we do or not is evident in our character, it is evident in the things we say and do.

Fellowship

> [1] Brethren, even if anyone is caught in any trespass, you who are spiritual, restore such a one in a spirit of gentleness; each one looking to yourself, so that you too will not be tempted. [2] Bear one another's burdens, and thereby fulfill the law of Christ. [3] For if anyone thinks he is something when he is nothing, he deceives himself. [4] But each one must examine his own work, and then he will have reason for boasting in regard to himself alone, and not in regard to another.   [5] For each one will bear his own load.
>
> [6] The one who is taught the word is to share all good things with the one who teaches him. [7] Do not be deceived, God is not mocked; for whatever a man sows, this he will also reap. [8] For the one who sows to his own flesh will from the flesh reap corruption, but the one who sows to the Spirit will from the Spirit reap eternal life. [9] Let us not lose heart in doing good, for in due time we will reap if we do not grow weary. [10] So then, while we have opportunity, let us do good to all people, and especially to those who are of the household of the faith.

In Acts chapter 2 we see that church growth was a result of the sharing of responsibilities for one another in the body as well as reaching out to others with the gospel. Paul encourages them to be generous with one another. Generosity is usually a good indication of one's grasp of

God's mercy. Those who love and give little in proportion to their means usually have little insight into how much God loves them. If they did, they would give much more.

Paul encourages generosity towards the elderly and backsliders, preachers and teachers, as well as all those in need. It is not easy to give in any one of these areas, but how one does so is a good measure of one's sense of freedom in Christ. A generous spirit is a free spirit in Jesus.

Final Warnings and Salvation – 6:11-18

Warning against Circumcision Party

> [11] See with what large letters I am writing to you with my own hand. [12] Those who desire to make a good showing in the flesh try to compel you to be circumcised, simply so that they will not be persecuted for the cross of Christ. [13] For those who are circumcised do not even keep the Law themselves, but they desire to have you circumcised so that they may boast in your flesh. [14] But may it never be that I would boast, except in the cross of our Lord Jesus Christ, through which the world has been crucified to me, and I to the world. [15] For neither is circumcision anything, nor uncircumcision, but a new creation. [16] And those who will walk by this rule, peace and mercy be upon them, and upon the Israel of God.

Verse 11: Paul writes this letter with his own hand (he usually dictates his letters), and the use of bold, large letters probably means that he is writing boldly for the sake of emphasis.

Verse 12-16: Here it is revealed that the Judaizers are basically cowards who want the prestige of religious leadership without the risk. To preach the cross is risky and unpopular. Legalism and circumcision are safe and place all of the burdens on the Galatians, none on the teachers (who did not even try to live by the tenets of legalism which was perfect law keeping).

Paul says that his boast is not in his converts but in what the cross has done for him (revealed his sinfulness, lostness and salvation in Jesus).

Circumcision or not does not change you, Christ changes you when you are united to Him, and God blesses all who are changed by Him. Circumcision was a sign of promise to come, Jesus was the one who was to come and in Him all the promises are fulfilled.

Final Farewell

[17] From now on let no one cause trouble for me, for I bear on my body the brand-marks of Jesus.

[18] The grace of our Lord Jesus Christ be with your spirit, brethren. Amen.

Paul wants no more accusations and lets the scars that he has born for Christ be a witness for his defense, and gives his final blessing.

This completes our study of the book of Galatians. I hope this has been a worthwhile experience in gaining greater insight into the gospel and God's love of people. Please check out our other Bible studies on the BibleTalk.tv website where you will find material that will help you "grow your faith; share your faith."

Mike Mazzalongo
April - 2015

BibleTalk.tv is an Internet Mission Work.

We provide textual Bible teaching material on our website and mobile apps for free. We enable churches and individuals all over the world to have access to high quality Bible materials for personal growth, group study or for teaching in their classes.

The goal of this mission work is to spread the gospel to the greatest number of people using the latest technology available. For the first time in history it is becoming possible to preach the gospel to the entire world at once. BibleTalk.tv is an effort to preach the gospel to all nations every day until Jesus returns.

The Choctaw Church of Christ in Oklahoma City is the sponsoring congregation for this work and provides the oversight for the BibleTalk ministry team. If you would like information on how you can support this ministry, please go to the link provided below.

bibletalk.tv/support

Printed in Great Britain
by Amazon